mommy

แม่

mae

daddy

พ่อ

pho

boy

เด็กผู้ชาย

dekphuchai

girl

เด็กผู้หญิง

dek phuying

1

one
หนึ่ง
nueng

2

two
สอง
song

3

three
สาม
sam

4

four
สี่
si

5

five

ห้า

ha

6

six

หก

hok

7

seven

เจ็ด

chet

8

eight

แปด

paet

9

nine

เก้า

kao

10

ten

สิบ

sip

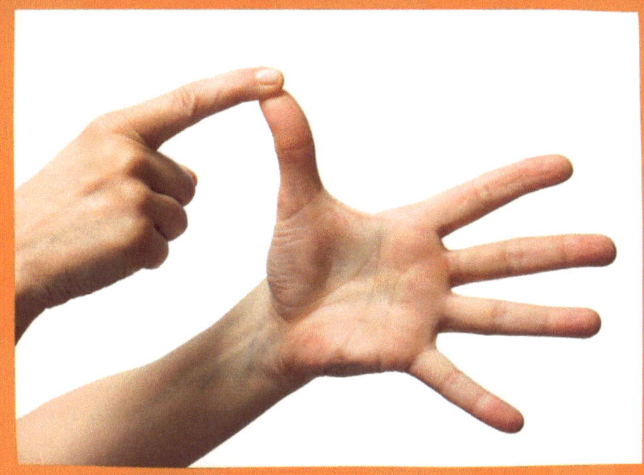

count

นับ

nap

write

เขียน

khian

draw

วาด

wat

paint

ระบาย

rabai

circle
วงกลม

wongklom

square
สีเหลียมจัตุรัส

siliamchatturat

rectangle
สีเหลียมผืนผ้า

siliamphuenpha

triangle
สามเหลียม

samliam

star

ดาว

dao

black

ดำ

dam

white

ขาว

khao

brown

น้ำตาล

namtan

red

แดง

daeng

blue

ฟ้า

fa

yellow

เหลือง

lueang

green

เขียว

khiao

purple
ม่วง
muang

gray
เทา
thao

orange
ส้ม
som

pink
ชมพู
chomphu

apple
แอปเปิ้ล
aeppoen

banana
กล้วย
kluai

pineapple
สับปะรด
sapparot

watermelon
แตงโม
taengmo

pear

แพร์

phae

grapes

องุ่น

angun

mango

มะม่วง

mamuang

peach

พีช

phicha

strawberry

สตรอว์เบอร์รี

sot ro boe ri

cherry

เชอร์รี

choeri

orange

ส้ม

som

coconut

มะพร้าว

maphrao

lemon
มะนาว
manao

mushroom
เห็ด
het

corn
ข้าวโพด
khaophot

tomato
มะเขือเทศ
makhueathet

pumpkin

ฟักทอง

fakthong

cucumber

แตงกวา

taengkawa

carrot

แครอท

khaerot

potato

มันฝรั่ง

manfarang

zucchini
ซุกินี
su kini

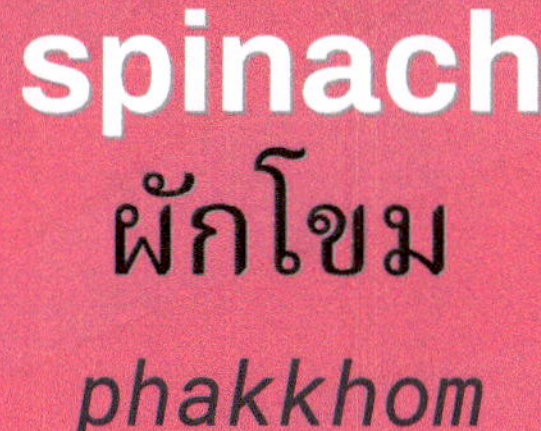

spinach
ผักโขม
phakkhom

cauliflower
กะหล่ำดอก
kalamdok

egg
ไข่
khai

plate
จาน

chan

spoon
ช้อน

chon

knife
มีด

mit

fork
ส้อม

som

cake
เค้ก

khek

baby bottle
ขวดนม

khuatnom

candies
ลูกอม

luk-om

cheese
ชีส

chit

drink
ดื่ม

duem

eat
กิน

kin

hot
ร้อน

ron

cold
เย็น

yen

small
เล็ก

lek

big
ใหญ่

yai

 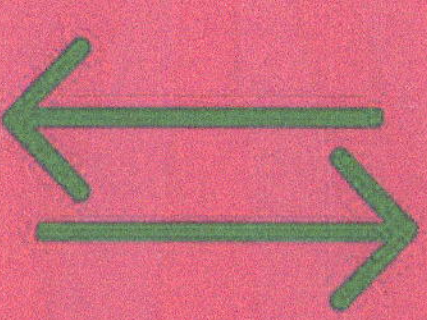 

short
สั้น

san

long
ยาว

yao

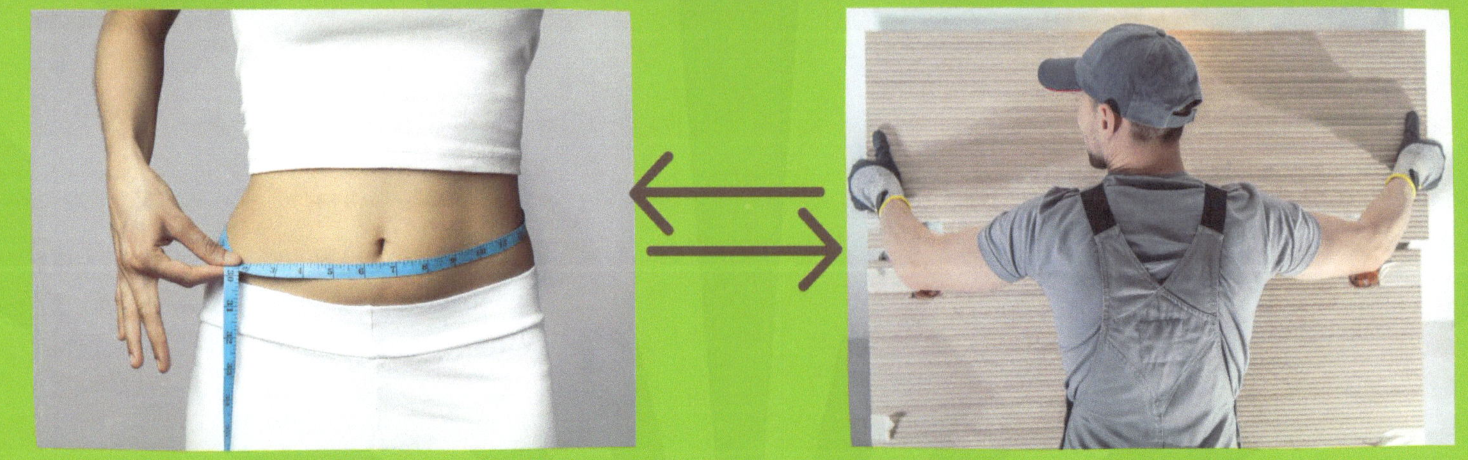

thin
บาง
bang

large
ใหญ่
yai

easy
ง่าย
ngai

difficult
ยาก
yak

stand up
ยืนขึน

yuen khuen

sit down
นั่งลง

nang long

sweet
หวาน

wan

salty
เค็ม

khem

heavy
หนัก
nak

light
เบา
bao

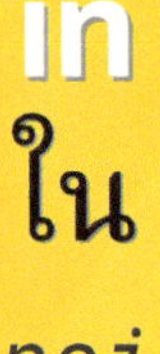

in
ใน
nai

out
นอก
nok

dirty
สกปรก
sokkaprok

clean
สะอาด
sa-at

close
ปิด
pit

open
เปิด
poet

pencils

ดินสอ

dinso

clock

นาฬิกา

nalika

key

กุญแจ

kunchae

book

หนังสือ

nangsue

bed
เตียง
tiang

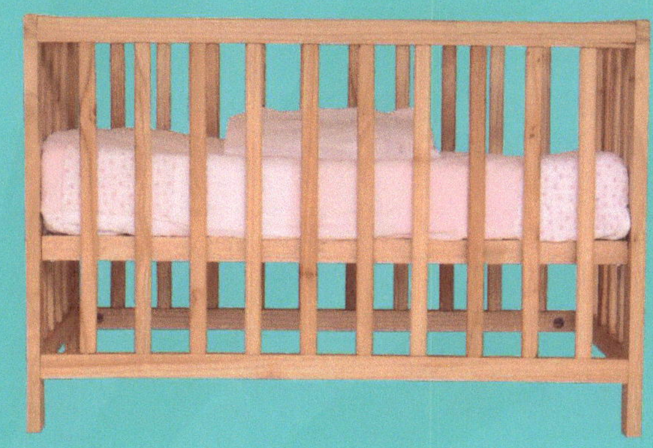

crib
เตียงเด็ก
tiangdek

table
โต๊ะ
to

chair
เก้าอี้
kao-i

car

รถยนต์

rotyon

bike

จักรยาน

chakkrayan

plane
เครื่องบิน

khrueangbin

boat
เรือ

ruea

train
รถไฟ

rotfai

helicopter
เฮลิคอปเตอร์

helikhoptoe

firetruck

รถดับเพลิง

rotdapphloeng

firefighter

พนักงานดับเพลิง

phanakngandapphloeng

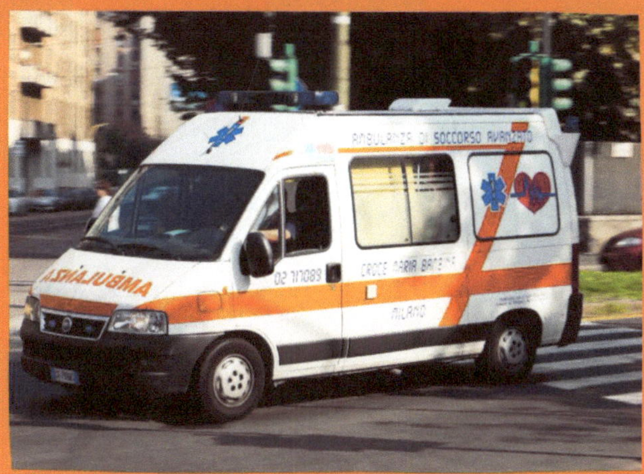

ambulance
รถพยาบาล

rotphayaban

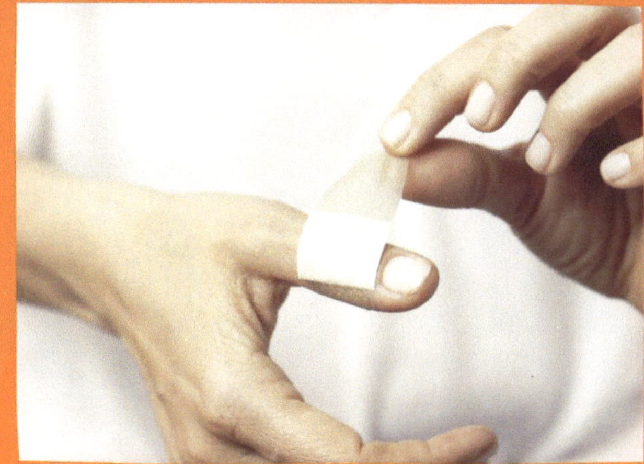

bandage
ผ้าพันแผล

phaphanphaen

paramedic
นักปฏิบัติการฉุกเฉินทางการแพทย์

nak pati bat kan chukchoen thangkan phaet

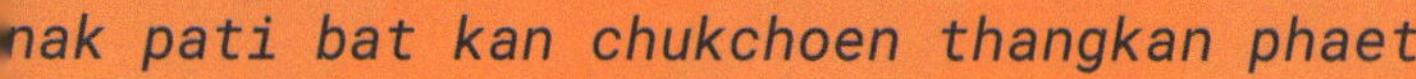

rescue team
ทีมกู้ภัย

thim kuphai

forest

ปา

pa

mountain

ภูเขา

phukhao

grass

หญ้า

ya

sand

ทราย

sai

tree
ต้นไม้

tonmai

flower
ดอกไม้

dokmai

butterfly
ผีเสื้อ

phisuea

ant
มด

mot

cat

แมว

maeo

dog

สุนัข

sunak

horse

ม้า

ma

mouse

หนู

nu

cow

วัว

wua

pig

หมู

mu

sheep

แกะ

kae

duck

เป็ด

pet

goose

ห่าน

han

rabbit

กระต่าย

kratai

fish

ปลา

pla

vet

สัตวแพทย์

sattawaphaet

doctor

หมอ

mo

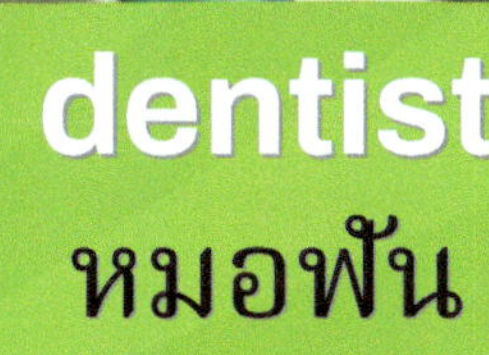

dentist

หมอฟัน

mofan

pharmacist

เภสัชกร

phesatchakon

nurse

พยาบาล

phayaban

head
หัว
hua

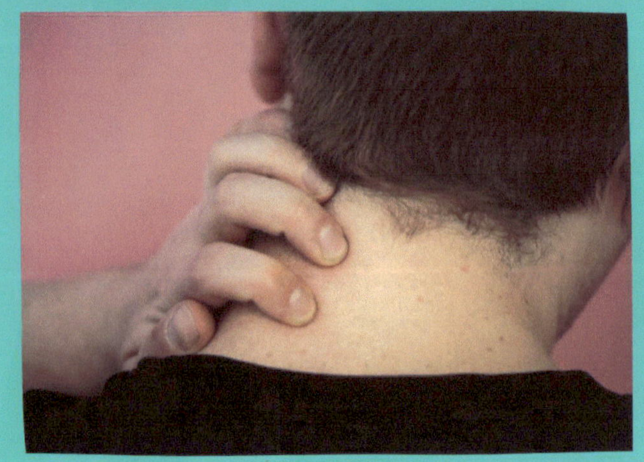

neck
คอ
kho

foot
เท้า
thao

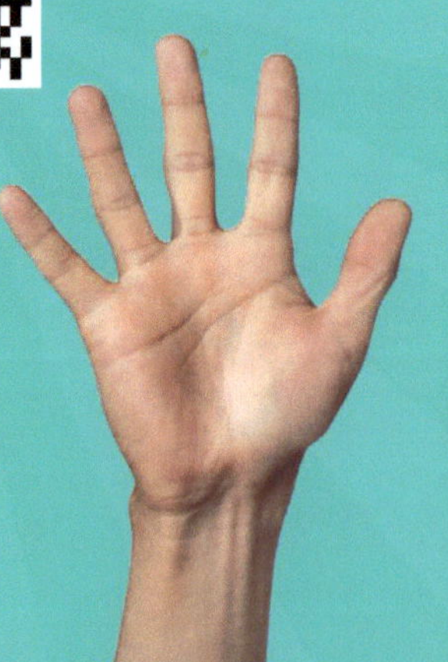

hand
มือ
mue

teeth

ฟัน

fan

eye

ตา

ta

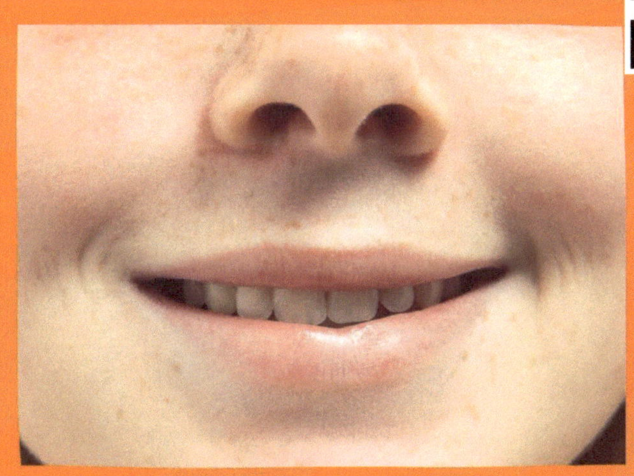

mouth

ปาก

pak

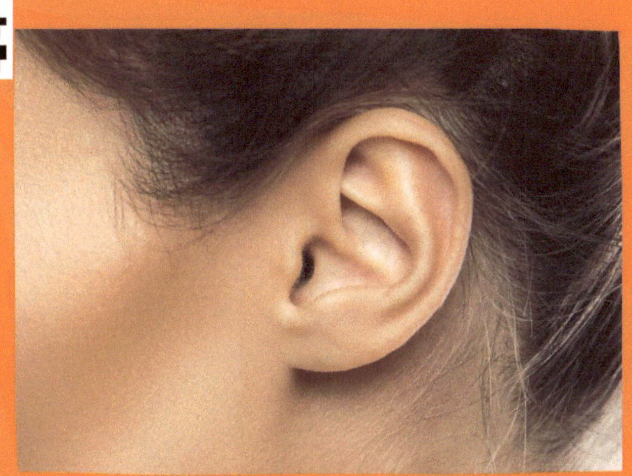

ear

หู

hu

hat
หมวก
muak

dress
ชุดกระโปรง
chut kraprong

pants
กางเกงขายาว
kangkengkhayao

shoes
รองเท้า
rongthao

coat
เสื้อโค้ท

suea khot

scarf
ผ้าพันคอ

phaphankho

umbrella
ร่ม

rom

glasses
แว่นตา

waenta

sun
ดวงอาทิตย์

duang-athit

cloudy
เมฆมาก

mekmak

rainy
ฝนตก

fontok

moon
ดวงจันทร์

duangchan